Metamorphosis
Greek Orthodox School
30 Scarsdale Road
Toronto, ON   M3B 2R7

D1539273

WOMEN
IN HISTORY

WOMEN AND THE FAMILY

Kate Hyndley

Wayland

WOMEN
IN HISTORY

Women and Business
Women and Education
Women and Literature
Women and Politics
Women and Science
Women and Sport
Women and the Arts
Women and the Family
Women and War
Women and Work

Series editor: Catherine Ellis
Consultant: Professor Deirdre Beddoe BA, PhD,
Dip Ed, Reader in History at The Polytechnic
of Wales
Designer: Michael Morey
Picture editor: Shelley Noronha

Front cover: Baby's Birthday, from a painting
by Hardy.
Back cover: Top left – Marie Stopes (1880–1958),
pioneer of methods of birth control. Top right – a
nurse and four children *c.* 1910. Bottom left – wartime
evacuees. Bottom right – child in an inner London
nursery.

First published in 1989 by
Wayland (Publishers) Limited
61 Western Road, Hove
East Sussex BN3 1JD, England

© Copyright 1989 Wayland (Publishers) Limited

British Library Cataloguing in Publication Data
Kate Hyndley
   Women and the family. – (Women in history
    (Wayland Publishers).
   1. Great Britain. Women. Family life.
   Effects of careers
   I. Title   II. Series
   305.4

   ISBN 1–85210–502–X

Typeset by Kalligraphics Limited, Horley, Surrey
Printed in Italy by G. Canale & C.S.p.A., Turin
Bound in the UK by Mac Lehose & Partners, Portsmouth

Picture acknowledgements
The pictures in this book were supplied by
the following: The Billie Love Collection back
cover top right, 17 (bottom); The Bridgeman
Art Library front cover; Family Planning
Association 41; Format Photographers 37, 38,
42, 43, 44; Gingerbread 39 (Beckenham &
Penge Advertiser); Girton College, Cambridge
17 (top); Richard and Sally Greenhill back
cover bottom right; Hulton Picture Library
back cover bottom left, 5, 6 (bottom), 7, 9, 12,
13 (bottom), 22, 30, 31, 32 (bottom), 36; Impe-
rial War Museum 23; John Frost Historical
Newspapers 4; The Mansell Collection 26;
Mary Evans back cover top left, 8, 10, 11, 13
(top), 14 (top), 15, 18 (The Fawcett Library),
19, 21 (top) (The Fawcett Library), 25 (both),
29; Peter Newark's Western Americana 16,
20; Topham 6 (top), 14 (bottom), 21 (bottom),
27, 28 (both), 32 (top), 33, 34, 35, 40.

Permissions
The publisher would like to thank the following
for allowing certain extracts to be used in the book:
Longman Group UK Ltd. for *Politics of Women's
Rights* by April Carter (1988); Virago Press for *Round
About a Pound a Week* by Maud Pember Reeves,
introduction by Sally Alexander (1979); Croom
Helm Ltd. for *Women in Europe since 1750* by Patricia
Branca (1978); Open University Press for *The
Changing Experience of Women, Unit 9 The Family*
(1983); BBC Books for *Out of the Doll's House* by
Angela Holdsworth (1988); Wheatsheaf Books Ltd.
for *Women in England 1870–1950* by Jane Lewis
(1984); Janet Dunbar for *Early Victorian Women*
(Harrap, 1953).

Contents

INTRODUCTION
page 4

1 A WOMAN'S PLACE
page 5

2 THE INDUSTRIAL AGE BEGINS 1800-1840
page 8

3 HOME AND HEARTH 1840-1870
page 13

4 VICTORIAN FAMILIES 1870-1900
page 17

5 MOTHERHOOD AND WAR 1900-1918
page 21

6 THE NATION'S HEALTH 1918-1938
page 27

7 WARFARE AND WELFARE 1939-1959
page 32

8 FAMILIES AND JOBS — THE DOUBLE
BURDEN – 1960 onwards
page 36

9 LOOKING FORWARD TO EQUALITY AT
HOME – the 1980s onwards
page 41

Projects – *page 45*
Books to read – *page 46*
Glossary – *page 46*
Index – *page 48*

Introduction

PERSIL–white goes further ahead!

PERSIL now contains 'RAYOL'—the wonderful new-life ingredient which makes Persil-white even whiter still! Persil's power to give brilliant snowy whiteness has *increased!* Its deep-cleansing suds, containing 'Rayol' — a marvellous new substance —

now give a *lasting*, radiant finish to white things. Persil gives new life to tired whites and a soft, lovely radiance to coloureds.

PERSIL—containing 'RAYOL'—washes whiter than ever!

r&s 1148-879-100

One plan you *must* make for their future

PLANNING your children's future, you would do *anything* to make your hopes come true. Don't overlook the everyday danger that may tragically cut that future short.

Nearly twenty children are killed on the roads each week. Many more are gravely injured. How can you keep your own youngsters safe?

Start tomorrow to teach them Kerb Drill—and keep on until they do it automatically, at every crossing. Next to your own guiding hand, this simple routine is their surest safeguard.

1. At the kerb, *halt!*
2. Eyes *right!*
3. Eyes *left!*
4. Glance again — *right!*
5. Then IF IT'S CLEAR — *quick march!* Don't rush. Cross calmly.

ISSUED BY THE MINISTRY OF TRANSPORT

HEALTH PLAN *keeps this family fit*

IF THERE WERE a prize for fitness, George and his Grandad would share it. A schoolboy and a man past sixty—they both benefit from their regular course of Scott's Emulsion. It's Mother's plan —throughout the year, she gives them Scott's Emulsion. This food tonic extra is rich in the fats and vitamins that a rationed diet lacks.

GEORGE AND GRANDAD—some good health—some good reason

People of all ages need the protective nourishment of Scott's Emulsion — cod liver oil in its most digestible form, with Vitamins A and D and Hypophosphites. Three tablespoonfuls a day

provide the fat and vitamin value of nearly two extra butter rations. Give your family Scott's Emulsion now; it will put them all in better shape to fight fatigue, and ward off infection.

Scott's Emulsion EVERY SPOONFUL LEADS TO BETTER HEALTH

Have families always been the same as they are today? The chapters of this book follow the changes that have taken place in women's daily lives in the family from 1800 until the present. It is a long step from the Victorian 'angel in the home' to today's working woman who combines a career with her role as mother. For most women the passage of time has brought a great deal more freedom and choice. The struggle to gain these improvements, most of which have been so recently won, forms the content of this book.

In the last century, women's lives were dominated by the constant demands of childbirth. In the 1870s, 66 per cent of women had five or more children, whereas today only 4 per cent have four or more children. As the birth rate dropped, some mothers became freer to work outside the home. However, most working-class women had been combining menial factory work and domestic responsibilities throughout the Industrial Revolution. Today women face a quite different set of problems. A higher divorce rate has led to an increasing number of mothers raising their families alone. Even with a partner, many women find the double burden of family responsibilities and a full-time job outside the home difficult to cope with.

It is hard to generalize, however, as in all the periods covered by this book there are huge differences between the lives of women in each social class. As women's lives change so does the family itself – both in its structure and in its organization. So what will the future hold? A look at the past may give some indication of the changes to come.

Advertisers have always tried to influence women, by assuming their main interests are home and family.

1

A Woman's Place

In earlier times the world outside the home was closed to women. Music, art and sewing were the acceptable outlets for a woman's talent.

Since time began the family has been central to women's lives. It has been the one sphere where a woman's influence and knowledge was allowed to be dominant. The phrase 'a woman's place is in the home' sums up the domestic role traditionally given to women. Throughout history there have always been some who challenged this narrow confinement within the family, but it was not until the second half of the twentieth century that wider opportunities became available to the majority of women.

The bulk of the work which goes on within the family – child-care, cooking, cleaning – has always been done by women. As this is still true, it is tempting to suggest that women's position within the family has not greatly changed over the two centuries this book covers. Closer inspection reveals that although women's lives are still generally centred around the family, the quality of their lives has changed dramatically.

There are three broad areas of change. Firstly, the extent to which women work outside the home and the type of work available to them. Secondly, the nature of domestic work itself and the labour-saving machinery used to assist with these tasks. Thirdly, and perhaps most important, the reduction in the number of children the average woman will bear and bring up during her lifetime. This has released women from family ties much earlier than in previous generations.

It is not simply that women now have fewer children, but that the children they do have tend to be born closer together in the earlier years of marriage. This, together with a longer life expectancy, means that a woman marrying in the late twentieth century will live for almost fifty years after the birth of her last child. A hundred years ago she would have had more children and would have been lucky to live twenty years after the last child's birth.

Housework is also much less of a burden than it was. Even basic facilities such as hot and cold running water, gas and electricity for cooking, heating and lighting were not generally

6

The family can provide women and men with many pleasurable and rewarding experiences; it can also be the source of much frustration, even pain – indeed it has been argued by some feminists that the family is a central, if not the greatest, source of women's oppression. From *The Changing Experience of Women*, 1983.

9

Right *Two washerwomen, c. 1900. Before the advent of hot and cold running water and washing machines, the weekly wash was an arduous task for poorer women.*

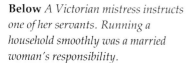

The ideal role . . . of 'superwoman' could hardly be more different from that offered nineteenth-century middle-class women, and yet very little has changed in respect to women's continued responsibility for home and family. Jane Lewis, *Women in England 1870-1950.*

Below *A Victorian mistress instructs one of her servants. Running a household smoothly was a married woman's responsibility.*

available until after the First World War. Washing machines, fridges and vacuum cleaners are even more recent additions to the household. Their existence allows women to consider other activities such as full or part-time employment. Some women wait until their children are old enough to be independent. Others prefer to return to work sooner.

Although attitudes to men and housework have changed a little, most household chores are still done by women, even if they also work outside the home. A recent survey by the Marriage Research Centre found that on average a woman did three-quarters of the work in the home, even in households where both partners worked full-time.

Nevertheless, the main change in women's lives over the last 200 years has been the extent to which they are able to work outside the home. The census of 1861 showed that a quarter of all women – 2.7 million – worked in paid employment. This was probably an under-estimate, as the census did not record *all* areas of women's work, including taking in washing or out-work. Out of these 2.7 million women, however, two million worked as domestic servants. Domestic service was still the largest single occupation for women until the Second World War. Today the picture is very different: women now make up 40 per cent of the workforce and work in a great variety of jobs.

The basic facts of the changes in women's experience of family life can be discovered by looking at statistics, but a clearer picture needs more information. To understand more about the changing status of women we need to look at social attitudes in the past and women's lack of legal rights, especially after marriage.

The servants of a large household in Victorian times. Domestic service was the main employment for women, well into the twentieth century.

Colliery workers from Lancashire. Women and children were often used as cheap labour in the mining industry, until public concern at their conditions of work led to legislation limiting their employment.

> **Most married women were burdened with many pregnancies. This did not, however, produce extraordinarily large families on the average. For family size was also regulated by the high rate of infant mortality and a large number of still births.**
> Patricia Branca, *Women in Europe Since 1750*, 1978.

2

The Industrial Age Begins

1800–1840

At the beginning of the nineteenth century Britain was experiencing a period of rapid social change. Industry was taking over from agriculture as the main way to make a living. As new towns and factories sprang up all over the country, large numbers of people left the countryside to work in the city. In 1801 only 20 per cent of the population lived in towns but by 1851 that figure had doubled. This huge upheaval is generally known as the Industrial Revolution and it changed the nature of family life forever.

Before the industrial age, life had remained unchanged for centuries. Most families lived by cultivating the land or by making goods in small-scale cottage industries. Women's work was essential to the family economy. Peasant families had to struggle to produce enough food for all their members. Married women had to be able to cope with hard physical labour, as well as the burdens of childbearing, often with little to eat. Children were also expected to work hard.

At this time women married quite late, at about 25–28 years, mainly because they could not afford to before this time. After marriage they spent, on average, fifteen years bearing between six and eight children, many of whom lived only a short time. Infant mortality was very high. Some estimates suggest as many as 50 per cent of babies died before the age of two. Many women died in childbirth. Motherhood as a full-time occupation was unheard of for poor women as they could not be spared from their work in the house and fields for long. Babies were fed when time allowed.

From 1750 onwards the domestic system of labour became more widespread. Raw materials would be taken to cottage workshops and the finished products collected later. Peasant women supplemented the family income by producing lace, buttons, gloves and by weaving wool and cotton cloth. Although this work was often poorly paid, it did allow women to combine family responsibilities with earning money. In poorer families working conditions in the home were often squalid and children had to work long hours to help their parents earn enough to live on.

After 1800, the new factories began to compete with the cottage industries, often forcing them out of business. Many families had little choice but to move to the towns and seek work in the factories and mills. This often meant the breakup of families and isolation from the wider network of relatives who had previously lived close by. Many women also found they were unable to combine work and child care, as the new jobs in the factory meant long hours away from home.

Women who had to work faced a grim prospect. Factory work was hard, and those with young children had to leave them with untrained childminders. Young babies were often dosed with opium-based syrups such as Godfrey's Cordial, to make them sleep while their mothers were working.

In spite of these problems, many working-class married women and their older children continued to work in factories, particularly in the textile trade. They were employed as weavers on the new power looms and were often used as cheap labour

Lace workers produce high quality goods in Devon, 1875. Although the work was highly skilled the women often worked long hours for low pay, as factory-produced goods kept prices low.

in preference to men. Even so, by 1841 only 25 per cent of female cotton workers were married, the rest were single girls, spinsters or widows. Married working-class women were often forced to earn money as cleaners, or by taking in laundry, which was easier to combine with their responsibilities at home.

For middle-class women the separation between home and work had a different effect. Instead of being drawn into work, they tended to be cut off from it and were more closely confined to the home. Many middle-class married women had taken an active role in a family business, such as running a shop. As these businesses prospered, a separate family home was often bought and the wife became less involved in the business as it was more difficult to combine with family life from a distance.

Children employed in the textile industry talk to a government factory inspector. Inspectors' reports of the time give a clear picture of the terrible conditions in the new factories.

New mills and factories were built in the midst of a rural landscape as the industrial age progressed.

Similarly, on large farms the wives would often take charge of the dairy and other produce. As farmers became richer during the nineteenth century their wives began to withdraw from such active involvement and became 'gentlewomen' with 'nothing to do'. This was in keeping with the socially acceptable role for middle-class women at this time.

This period brought fewer changes to the lives of upper-class women. They were spared the hard physical labour and poor nutrition that the majority of women had to endure. Domestic servants freed richer married women from housework and child care, although they often spent a lot of time organizing their households. There were, however, two ways in which the lives of rich and poor women were alike. The first was in the dangers and discomfort of childbearing. Although with better nutrition the number of infant and maternal deaths at birth were fewer in richer families, they were still very high indeed. This was mainly because there was so little understanding of the dangers of infection.

The second problem which all married women shared during this period was their legal status. Married women were not recognized in law as being separate from their husbands; in fact, they were their husbands' property. A wife had no protection from her husband if he was violent towards her, no right to maintenance if he deserted her, and no right to divorce. Worst of all, women had no rights at all over their own children, not even the right to visit them if a marriage broke up. During the nineteenth century, women began to object to these laws and a few brave women fought hard to get them changed. Caroline Norton was one of them.

❛
I used to be employed... in driving bullocks to the field and fetching them again... pulling turnips and anything that came to hand. I got up at five or six, except on market mornings twice a week, and then at three. I went to bed at half-past nine. A nine-year-old girl's account of her working day, 1843.
❜

Caroline Norton (1808–1877)

Caroline Norton was the beautiful and talented granddaughter of Sheridan, the playwright. She had no strong feelings about women's rights in general. She was drawn by her own bitter experience into the fight to change the law which gave mothers no rights over their own children.

As a young woman of eighteen she married George Norton, who was ten years her senior. It was not a happy marriage and when George was drunk he hit Caroline. This disgusted her family, but legally there was nothing she or they could do to stop it.

Instead, Caroline coped by writing poems and articles for society magazines and surrounding herself with literary friends. She earned a considerable amount of money by publishing her work, which was unusual for a woman at that time. George and Caroline were drawn closer together by their love for their children – Fletcher, who was born in 1829, and Brinsley, born in 1831. After their third son arrived in 1833, however, they began to have violent quarrels. Following one of these fights, Caroline left the house and later found to her horror that in her brief absence the three children had been taken away to their uncle's house. She soon discovered that George was quite within his legal rights to prevent her from seeing them again.

George Norton did not look after the children, but sent them to an estate in Scotland where they were cared for haphazardly by servants. Caroline was heart-broken by the separation from her children, and in desperation began to try to change the law. She wrote pamphlets and enlisted the help of political friends to get a bill introduced into Parliament. Eventually, in 1839, the Infants' Custody Act was passed, allowing children under the age of seven to reside with their mother if she was of 'good character'. However, the Bill did not help Caroline Norton as her children were in Scotland, which was not affected by the new law.

In 1842 Caroline's youngest son was tragically killed in a riding accident. After the funeral Caroline's husband relented and let the two older boys (by this time aged thirteen and eleven) go home to their mother. Caroline Norton's campaign helped many other women to keep their children after separating from their husbands.

Caroline Norton – she began the fight for women to have legal rights over their own children.

3

Home and Hearth

1840–1870

During the Victorian era (1837–1901) the family was considered to be the most important part of the social structure. In a rapidly changing industrial world, the family represented stability. A woman's role was clearly stated. Her aim was to marry and have children; no alternative occupations were considered sufficiently respectable. Those who did not marry were often pitied and ridiculed.

Once married, a woman attempted to become the 'perfect

Above Punch *cartoon, 'Parents of ten, parents often.'* **Below** *Upper-class Victorian children being presented to their parents before dinner.*

Above *A woman washes clothes using a peg-dolly to churn the laundry.*

wife'. She had to be obedient to her husband, and have no strong ideas of her own – in fact 'the angel in the home'. The only suitable interests for a Victorian middle-class woman were those connected with the family and the home. The perfect wife was expected to be ignorant of the outside world and was sheltered from the grimmer realities of Victorian England.

This model of the family obviously did not tally with the realities of life for many working-class women. Their lives were so hard that the luxury of bringing up a family without having to work was impossible.

Many women strove to follow the example of Queen Victoria, who was at this time a young wife herself, raising a large family. Marriage was considered a serious business and there were many manuals available on the subject of how to 'get' and keep a husband. One of the most popular writers of the time was Mrs Ellis, whose first book *Daughters of England* (published in 1845) explained that a woman's 'highest duty is so often to suffer and be still'. This passive role was to affect women's lives for many years to come. However, at the same time some small progress was being made on the legal front. In 1857, the first reforms of the divorce laws were made with the Matrimonial Cause Bill. This allowed a man to divorce his wife on grounds of her adultery. A woman had to show additional misconduct by her husband as well as his adultery! Nevertheless, divorce was now possible and the Bill also gave women some rights to keep their own property on separation from their husbands.

The practical reality of running a Victorian home was a long

Right *A young scullery maid helps prepare the meal. Cooking with coal was dirty, and the kitchen range and the pots and pans required a lot of maintenance.*

way from the ideals discussed above. For most working-class women the physical effort involved in housework was very hard indeed. Coal was the main fuel used for heating and cooking, and this meant a lot of dirt and soot to clean away. Cooking was usually done on a kitchen range. The fire at the centre of the hearth was boxed in to form a hot plate, with an oven to one side and another square metal box on the other side to act as a boiler for hot water. The chimney and flues had to be cleaned regularly and every morning the range had to be cleaned, black-leaded, polished and lit before any cooking could be done.

The running of a Victorian household was such hard work that domestic help was essential (for those who could afford it). A comfortable middle-class family had several servants who did most of the heavy, manual work. Cleaning and washing took up a lot of time and energy. The water supply was often inadequate and in country areas water had to be pumped and carried from a well. Even in towns it was not common for each house to have its own tap – there would often be a tap for each street. In a working-class home, washing was usually done on a Monday, as there would be left-over cold meat from Sunday dinner, so no meal had to be prepared. In middle-class households with servants, a copper (a tank with a fire grate under it) was used for washing. This helped by providing hot water. The clothes were scrubbed in a wash tub, either rectangular to use with a fluted washboard or barrel-shaped to use with a peg dolly. This was a pole with prongs at the end, which was used to churn the washing around the tub.

There were many attempts to design a washing machine during the nineteenth century, but none was very successful. Washing remained a back-breaking task well into the twentieth century. Ironing was also a major task in Victorian times, especially as clothes were often very elaborate with many frills. Most irons were simply heated on the grate, but towards the end of this period spirit and petrol irons became more common.

Sanitation was generally very primitive in Victorian homes, and there was no mains drainage. Where sewage pipes existed they were usually unglazed and therefore leaky. This caused outbreaks of cholera and there were several epidemics of the disease in the 1840s.

There was a great deal of poverty in Victorian England due to unemployment and inadequate wages. Those families who could not support themselves could apply to the Poor Law Commissioners for help. Until 1834 'poor relief' was provided to 'deserving' families. This was known as 'outdoor relief',

> **'** *It was the Victorian era that encouraged the narrowest ideal of femininity... demanding from women gentility and domesticity. But at the very time this image of womanliness was being promoted a feminist movement was also being born.* April Carter, *The Politics of Women's Rights.* **'**

Overcrowding and poor sanitation caused disease to spread quickly in the towns. Epidemics of cholera and other infections killed large numbers of people.

BOARD OF WORKS
FOR THE LIMEHOUSE DISTRICT.
COMPRISING LIMEHOUSE, RATCLIFF, SHADWELL & WAPPING.

In consequence of the appearance of **CHOLERA** within this District, the Board have appointed the under-mentioned Medical Gentlemen who will give ADVICE, MEDICINE, AND ASSISTANCE, FREE OF ANY CHARGE, AND UPON APPLICATION, AT ANY HOUR OF THE DAY OR NIGHT.

The Inhabitants are earnestly requested not to neglect the first symptoms of the appearance of Disease, (which in its early stage is easy to cure), but to apply, WITHOUT DELAY, to one of the Medical Gentlemen appointed.

The Board have opened an Establishment for the reception of Patients, in a building at Green Bank, near Wapping Church, (formerly used as Wapping Workhouse), where all cases of Cholera and Diarrhœa will be received and placed under the care of a competent Resident Medical Practitioner, and proper Attendants.

THE FOLLOWING ARE THE MEDICAL GENTLEMEN TO BE APPLIED TO;—

Mr. ORTON,
56, White Horse Street.

Dr. NIGHTINGALL,
4. Commercial Terrace, Commercial Road, (near Limehouse Church.)

Mr. SCHROEDER,
53, Three Colt Street, Limehouse.

Mr. HARRIS,
5, York Terrace, Commercial Road, (opposite Stepney Railway Station.)

Mr. CAMBELL,
At Mr. GRAY's, Chemist, Old Road, opposite "The World's End."

Mr. LYNCH,
St. James's Terrace, Back Road, Shadwell.

Mr. HECKFORD,
At the Dispensary, Wapping Workhouse.

By Order.
BOARD OFFICES, WHITE HORSE STREET,   THOS. W. RATCLIFF,
26th July, 1866.   *Clerk to the Board.*

The bible is read to the inmates of a London night refuge. Life was hard for those without employment and poverty was widespread.

which meant that the family was helped while living in their own home. In 1834, owing to the rising cost of assisting such people, the New Poor Law came into existence. This stated that able-bodied men and their families would no longer be offered 'outdoor relief'. If they wanted help they had to go into the workhouse – this was known as 'indoor relief'. Once inside the workhouse, families were split up.

The workhouse was built in four separate sections: one for men, one for women, one for boys and one for girls. Within each section the inmates lived and worked together with no privacy, and they were allowed no contact with other members of their family. Young children could often stay with their mothers, but children over seven were taken away. All inmates, including children over seven years, had to work ten hours a day.

There were some exceptions who were still allowed outdoor relief, but this depended on the good-will of the local Board of Guardians. Widows with young children and deserted wives qualified for this help. However, a woman could be refused outdoor relief if she had an illegitimate child, took in male lodgers, or even failed to keep her house and children clean. As the century went on, many private charities were set up and they began to provide an alternative source of help to the Poor Law and the workhouse. Even these charities, however, were anxious to help only the 'deserving poor'.

Because the assistance given to the poor was so inadequate, many families faced unimaginable hardship. But in Victorian times, a destitute family did not have the same sacred importance as a well-to-do middle-class family.

6 ━━━━━━━━━

Writers like Mrs Ellis made it quite clear what was expected: softness and weakness, delicacy and modesty... an endearing ignorance of everything that went on beyond household and social life. Husbands demanded charm, a high sense of domestic duty, admiration for and submission to themselves... Janet Dunbar, *The Early Victorian Woman.*

━━━━━━━━━ 9

4

Victorian Families

1870–1900

Towards the end of the nineteenth century, pressure to change women's inferior social, legal and political position began to increase. The demand for women to be given the vote was well under way, even though it was not achieved until after the First World War (1914–1918). Some legal progress was achieved in this period. In 1882, largely as a result of the tireless campaign by Barbara Bodichon, the Married Women's Property Act was eventually passed by Parliament. This, and another act in 1893, gave women the right to own and control their own property and income after marriage. The Act meant a major improvement in women's position because it allowed them financial independence from their husbands within marriage.

In 1886, women gained further rights over their children when the Guardianship of Infants Act became law. This allowed a woman to become the guardian of her own children after her husband's death. Before this a father had sole control over his

Above *Barbara Bodichon – her campaign to allow women to keep their own property after marriage succeeded in 1882.*

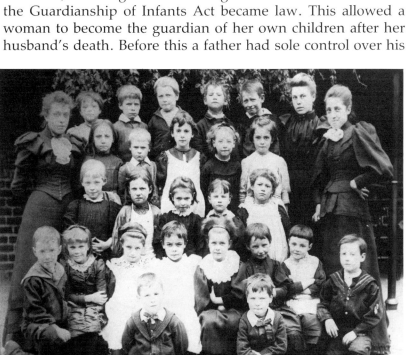

Left *Elementary schools became compulsory for children in 1880.*

The first students at Lady Margaret Hall, Oxford – a new college for women opened in 1879. Girton College, Cambridge, founded in 1869, was the first women's university college.

children and could, if he wished, leave them to the guardianship of a stranger when he died rather than to their own mother!

In education, too, progress was being made. In 1880 elementary schooling was made compulsory. This changed the role of children because they became an economic liability rather than useful contributors to the family income. Nevertheless, it eased the burden of mothers who no longer had to supervise their school-age children during the day. Concern was growing over the quality of education offered to middle-class girls. There were many private schools for 'young ladies', but they taught only domestic skills and 'accomplishments'. The first academic schools for girls were set up in the 1850s by Miss Buss who founded the North London Collegiate School for Ladies, and Miss Beale who opened the Cheltenham Ladies College.

A clearer picture of what life was like for women at the end of the nineteenth century can be gained by looking at two contrasting personal accounts of family life at this time. Molly Hughes' book, *A London Child of the 1870s*, describes her experience of growing up in a comfortable middle-class home. Her father was a stockbroker and the family lived in a large house in Canonbury, north London. Molly had a happy childhood and along with her four brothers enjoyed a good deal of freedom. They had a large, warm playroom with a huge table and lots of books. The family also had several servants.

Although Molly Hughes' mother was a lively and open-minded woman, Molly's life was far more restricted than that of her brothers. In order to prevent Molly becoming spoilt, her

Obviously in [my mother's] scheme of things men were the important people – well they are. And I shall never cease to be grateful to her for training me from childhood to appreciate this point. Molly Hughes, *A London Girl of the 1880's.*

Many poor women with families worked in their own homes in order to scratch a living. This woman is making boxes in the East End of London.

mother devised a 'boys first' rule. Molly explains just what this meant:

'I came last in all distribution of food at table, treats of sweets and so on. I was expected to wait on the boys, run messages, fetch things left upstairs, and never grumble, let alone refuse.'

The boys also went on many excursions, trips to the theatre and music hall, visits to exhibitions and shows, but Molly was always excluded from these outings. The reason for this was that it was not considered suitable for a young woman to know much about life outside the home. Molly describes her own father's attitude:

'My father's slogan was that boys should go everywhere and know everything and that a girl should stay at home and know nothing.'

Despite these restrictions Molly Hughes later gained a good education, travelled widely, and became a pioneer in the setting up of teacher training for women.

Arthur Harding's experience of childhood in the East End of London in the 1890s is a great contrast to the comfortable life enjoyed by the Hughes family. Harding's mother was disabled, but still managed to support the family by working at home making matchboxes for the Bryant and May company. She had to make nearly 100 boxes a day to earn enough to survive, and the boxes had to be spread over the floor to dry. As the family of five lived in only one room, measuring 3 metres by 3.6 metres, there was no room for the children indoors. They played out in the street after school.

> **You've got to remember this, that young or old, the mother was the top johnny in the family. What she said was law. All the money you earned went to her and she would share it out.** Raphael Samuel, *East End Underworld*, 1981.

Harding's mother was a great survivor and knew how to make the most of local charities. She always made sure the children looked poor (but clean) and wore clothes that didn't fit, so that they would be given new ones. The church mission was next door to the school and the children were given their breakfast at the mission – provided that they attended Sunday school. Lunch was a matter of snatching whatever they could. One church gave a jam pudding to the children, but if they missed that they had to beg from shopkeepers or passers-by. In the evening, Arthur Harding's mother always made a good stew to fill them all up.

At one point Harding's family were thrown out of their lodgings and slept under the railway arches until some dockers took pity on them and told them where they could find a room. Arthur Harding describes how difficult it was to wash clothes when they lived at the top of the house and there was only a tap in the yard:

'The most terrible instrument of torture that ever was invented for a poor family was the great big bath what they done the washing in. They'd stand for hours, washing – hard, terrible hard work.'

Arthur Harding was sent to a Dr Barnardo's home at nine years of age because there was no room for him at home.

During the Victorian period people gradually became more aware of the terrible conditions in which the poor had to live. Some, like Octavia Hill, spent much of their lives attempting to improve the housing available to poor families. By buying up, improving and managing property she was able to offer decent rented accommodation to ordinary families as an alternative to slum dwellings.

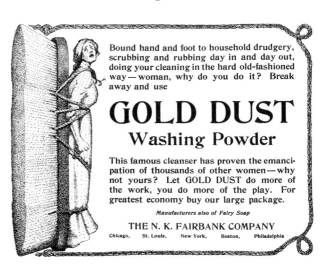

Bound hand and foot to household drudgery, scrubbing and rubbing day in and day out, doing your cleaning in the hard old-fashioned way – woman, why do you do it? Break away and use

GOLD DUST
Washing Powder

This famous cleanser has proven the emancipation of thousands of other women – why not yours? Let GOLD DUST do more of the work, you do more of the play. For greatest economy buy our large package.

Manufacturers also of Fairy Soap

THE N. K. FAIRBANK COMPANY
Chicago,   St. Louis,   New York,   Boston,   Philadelphia

Emancipation through washing powder? Successive generations of women found it was not as simple as this advertisement claims.

5

Motherhood and War

1900–1918

By 1900, Britain had begun to experience a challenge to its position as a world leader, both as a manufacturer and as an international military power. As the first industrial nation Britain had become the 'workshop of the world' and enjoyed the prosperity which followed. Now, this was challenged by the Germans and Americans whose own industries were providing new competition. On the military front Britain's confidence had been shaken by the failure to win the Boer War.

As a result of these signs of economic and military weakness,

Above *a woman operating railway signals*. **Below** *members of the Women's Territorial Signalling Corps.*

attitudes to mothers and the children they produced began to change. There was national concern about the birth rate which had already begun to fall, and the infant mortality rate. The number of babies who died at birth or before they reached their first birthday was still very high at this time – 160 deaths per thousand live births – and it had been at this level throughout the nineteenth century. It was not until the early years of the twentieth century that the number of infant deaths began to fall. People began to feel that it was a matter of social importance that a large and healthy new generation was produced, both as a workforce and as potential members of the armed forces.

In 1908, as a result of these new attitudes, the Liberal Government was able to introduce social reforms. They introduced old age pensions, school meals and school medical inspections for the first time. These were followed in 1911 by the National Insurance Act which allowed wage earners who had paid their contributions to the scheme access to free medical services. Although this was a great step forward it still left women and children without medical provision. The Act did include a 30 shilling maternity benefit, but this only covered a doctor's services at the actual birth. Outside this there was no health

Women working in an engineering workshop in 1917. Although they learned new skills, few were allowed to use them after the war.

Work in the munitions factories involved long hours and contact with dangerous chemicals.

care for mothers unless they could pay the very high costs.

At this time the Women's Co-operative Guild, under the leadership of Margaret Llewellyn Davies, began to campaign for a better deal for mothers. In order to find out more about the conditions facing the Guild's 32,000 members, Miss Davies invited women to write to her describing their own experiences of motherhood. The letters sent in reply presented a vivid picture of suffering and hardship among mothers – and these were the wives of skilled manual labourers who earned better-than-average wages.

The women who wrote in described the large number of miscarriages and stillbirths they endured, the lack of medical care, the unremitting hard physical work throughout each pregnancy and their inadequate nutrition as they economized on their own food to provide essentials for their families. As a result of these factors many babies died unnecessarily. When the letters were published in a book in 1915 – *Maternity: Letters from Working Women* – they shocked many readers and this helped the Guild to gain fresh support for its continued campaign to get proper ante-natal and mothercraft services provided by local authorities.

Another group concerned about the plight of poor families during this period was the Fabian Women's Group. Maud Pember Reeves and other socialist members conducted a survey of the daily lives of working class families living in Lambeth between 1909 and 1913. A report of their work was published in a book called *Round About a Pound a Week,* as this was the average income of the families they investigated. The survey was very detailed, and each mother was asked to give her

6

The conclusions were inescapable – the cause of infant mortality was not that mothers were ignorant or degenerate, but that they had too little money to provide for their own and their families' essential needs. Introduction by Sally Alexander to Maud Pember Reeves, *Round About a Pound a Week*, republished in 1979.

9

weekly budget as well as menus showing exactly what the family members ate.

Not only did they live in poor housing – husband, wife and four or five children living in two rooms – but the money left after the rent was paid was not enough to provide a good diet for all. As a result most menus showed the husband eating extra food, and nearly all the protein, while the wife and children lived almost entirely on bread and margarine washed down with tea. Cramped accommodation and poor nutrition led to much ill-health, but medical services were beyond the means of these families. The Fabian Women's Group campaigned for state support for poor families and, in particular, for an allowance for mothers which would give women some economic independence from their husbands. Despite the increased awareness of women's problems these issues were soon overshadowed by a greater threat – the First World War.

During the war, women began to work in jobs that had traditionally been done by men. At first this was resisted by employers and unions and there was therefore only a limited change. By 1915 women were replacing men in offices and in transport. The women who took on these new jobs were generally those who had been employed before the war in more traditional jobs, for instance in domestic service or the dressmaking industry. When conscription for men was introduced in January 1916, however, women were needed in greater numbers and began to take jobs in engineering, munitions factories and heavy industry. By this time married women were working too, making up 40 per cent of the female working population.

Although women who took on 'men's jobs' were paid less than the men would have earned, they were still able to take home a better wage than they would have been paid before the war. For this reason, despite the hard work, women were often healthier during the war because they were better fed. Many people disapproved of women with children working, even for the war effort. They argued that infant mortality and child neglect would rise as a result. In fact, evidence from the National Society for the Prevention of Cruelty to Children (NSPCC) showed a drop in both during the war years. Nevertheless, it was a widely-voiced opinion that by working outside the home, women were neglecting their true role as wives and mothers.

The First World War gave many women their first experience of work and broadened their view of the world. For some, the attractions of the home and family as a lifelong pursuit became much less appealing.

Women have done some wonderful work, but a baby is more wonderful than a machine gun. I believe that the hand that rocks the cradle will still be a power when the other is only a hateful memory. Mary Macarthur, *Daily News*, 1917.

The demand for birth control and smaller families grew after the First World War. This was the first clinic offering free contraceptive advice, opened by Marie Stopes in 1921.

Before war broke out the size of families had already begun to fall as men and women wanted to limit the number of children they had to support on meagre incomes. The methods of birth control available to them were very restricted, however. After the war, the poor conditions to which soldiers returned increased the demand for reliable ways to prevent conception. Marie Stopes was one of the pioneers in this field.

Marie Stopes (1880–1958)

On 17 March 1921 Marie Stopes opened the first birth control clinic in England. The aim of the birth control movement was for married women to be able to control how many children they had. Although many men used the condom at this time, there was no reliable device which women could use without their husband's co-operation.

Marie Stopes was an intelligent and energetic woman. In 1905 she became the youngest Doctor of Science in England and she was the first woman lecturer on the scientific staff of Manchester University. In 1911 she married Dr Reginald Gates, but the marriage was annulled in 1916 on grounds of non-consummation. As a result of her experience Marie Stopes wrote *Married Love*, published in 1918, which discussed how sex problems in a marriage could be solved. At this time the idea that a woman might enjoy sex was very shocking. However, the book proved to be very popular and was quickly followed by *Wise Parenthood* which contained a guide to contraceptive methods.

As a result of the success of this book Marie Stopes and her second husband, Humphrey Roe, opened the Mother's Clinic for Constructive Birth Control at 61 Marlborough Road, Holloway. The Clinic offered free consultations to poor women, and contraceptives at cost price. Marie Stopes aimed to help women avoid unwanted pregnancies and so allow them to enjoy both sex and motherhood. By the summer of 1924, 5,000 women had attended the Clinic.

There was considerable opposition from the medical profession because the Clinic did not rely on gynaecologists. Instead, it

Marie Stopes – she wanted to free women from the burden of unwanted pregnancies.

used trained nurses, as Marie Stopes felt women would be less intimidated by them. In addition many religious groups, particularly the Catholic Church, were very hostile to the new Clinic.

Ironically, Marie Stopes herself had difficulty conceiving a child but at last, aged 42, she gave birth to her only son, Harry, whom she adored. She believed sincerely, if misguidedly, that birth control would 'improve the race' as it would enable fewer and 'better quality' childen to be born. Although the first Clinics attracted relatively few patients, they set the scene for the continuing campaign for better birth control.

6

The Nation's Health

1918–1938

With women voting on the same footing as men for the first time, this Labour Party election poster shows how politicians now had to compete to attract the 'new voter'.

When the First World War ended, women who had worked in factories and munitions industries were expected to give up their jobs and return to their homes. Many women knew that the jobs they had done during the war gave better pay and conditions than those traditionally available to women, so they were reluctant to resign. In fact, only half of those who had taken up jobs during the war withdrew voluntarily. The rest were laid off as government contracts came to an end.

Public opinion was now firmly against women working, especially in 'men's jobs'. Some women did qualify for unemployment pay but this was stopped if they refused a job in laundry or domestic service. These jobs involved very long hours and pay which was often lower than the unemployment benefit given. Domestic service was particularly unpopular after the war, but women who needed employment were forced to accept it as there was no other work open to them. By 1921 there were as many women in domestic service as there had been before the war.

The idea that women should give up their jobs to 'male breadwinners' was particularly unfair to those whose husbands had been killed or permanently disabled in the war. Also, as so many young men had been killed there was a significant number of young women who could not expect to marry. And yet they were also excluded from decent jobs. So although war work initially broadened women's horizons, they were quickly narrowed again as soon as the war ended. Women went back into their homes, and if they did not have a home to go to they were automatically expected to become a servant in someone else's.

In legal terms, however, women's position did improve after the war. The most important change was that women were given the vote in 1919, although they had to be thirty before they were eligible. In 1928 the age restriction was withdrawn and for the first time women were given the same voting rights as men.

Above *Nursery schools were rare between the wars. This one in Peckham was opened by Lady Astor MP in 1935.*

In family law too there were significant changes. In 1923, the Matrimonial Causes Act allowed women to obtain a divorce on the same grounds as men. In 1937, desertion was added to the accepted reasons for ending a marriage. In 1925 a new Guardianship of Infants Act gave women equal guardianship rights over their children for the first time. At last, after more than eighty years, Caroline Norton's full demands for access to children had been granted.

There had also been some attempts to improve the well-being of mothers and their babies. In 1918, the Maternity and Child Welfare Act gave local authorities powers to set up ante-natal and child welfare clinics. This was one of a series of measures that had been taken to reduce the infant mortality rate which, between the turn of the century and 1920, had halved to 80 per thousand live births. The training of midwives had been more rigorous and the number of health visitors in England more than doubled during the years of the First World War. Local authorities were also allowed to set up milk depots which sold milk for infants at cost price.

Nevertheless, there was still great concern over the physical condition of the nation's population. Of every nine men conscripted between 1917 and 1918 only three were considered healthy, two more were sickly and the rest were physical wrecks. Public attention, however, was still directed at the health of babies rather than their mothers. The effect of this was that between 1923 and 1933 maternal mortality per thousand live births actually rose by 22 per cent.

Right *With mass unemployment during the thirties, many families had to survive on dole of £2.7s.6d.*

The Little Knob that does the work!

"This little knob means hours of leisure to me. I set it and leave it to do the cooking for me."

No other Cooker has this wonderful PARKINSON heat controller.

See the NEW SUBURBIA at your local Gas Company's showrooms, or write for the illustrated booklet.

The PARKINSON NEW SUBURBIA
GAS COOKER

THE PARKINSON STOVE CO., LTD., Stechford, BIRMINGHAM
London Showrooms: 8 & 10, GROSVENOR GARDENS, S.W.1.
And at GLASGOW—MANCHESTER—DUBLIN—BELFAST.

Revolutionary new cookers like this one, with thermostatic controls introduced in 1928, were available only to the most affluent families. The shortage of domestic servants made the new gadgets more popular.

Conditions for women within the family were still very poor in the inter-war years. Unless they were rich enough to afford domestic help and private medical care, their lives were often dominated by overwork and ill-health. Many groups were still campaigning for the provision of proper health care for women. Margery Spring Rice's book *Working Class Wives*, published in 1939, is the summary of a questionnaire survey conducted by the Women's Health Enquiry Committee. One and a quarter thousand married women were interviewed by their health visitors about their housing conditions, number of children, their working day, diet and health. The survey found that one

> **6**
>
> *The emancipation for which many thousand women have worked in the last hundred years, has had little or no effect on the domestic slavery of mind and body of the millions with whom rest the immediate care of a home and family.*
> Margery Spring Rice, *Working Class Wives*, 1939.
> **9**

Despite having won the vote, there was still a lot to be done for women to ensure equality. Here Eleanor Rathbone addresses a meeting as part of her campaign for Family Allowances.

third of the women were in good health, one third never felt well, and the remaining third had periodic bad health. They suffered from anaemia, bad teeth and gynaecological problems among other complaints, but only thirteen of the sample had access to a free doctor under the National Insurance Scheme.

Most of the women rarely consulted a doctor despite persistent bad health simply because it was too expensive. Doctors often advised them to get more rest, better nourishment, and more fresh air, but all of these were unavailable to the women. The survey also found that contraceptive advice was virtually non-existent, although there were some birth control clinics by this time. Doctors did not give advice on contraception, even after they had told women that more child-bearing would be dangerous for them.

The survey also showed that life for women with large families and poor living conditions was so hard that only the strongest could maintain good health. Homes often had only the most basic facilities, and many women still had to carry cold water up two flights of stairs and empty it again. There was still no hot water and the task of washing clothes was no easier than it had been in the previous century.

As a result of these conditions and increasing public awareness of them, the campaigns for better birth control and proper health care for all became dominant at this time. In addition, many women were arguing for an improvement in the conditions women and children faced, by the provision of family allowances to alleviate poverty and give women some financial independence. Eleanor Rathbone was one of the most enthusiastic supporters of family allowances.

Eleanor Rathbone (1872–1946)

The Rathbones were a wealthy shipping family from Liverpool. They were deeply involved in charity work and social reform. Eleanor Rathbone did not marry, but went to Oxford University in 1893. When she returned she worked with the Charity Organization Society which brought her into contact with many poor families in Liverpool.

Eleanor Rathbone was a feminist who fought to improve women's rights. She felt very strongly that a woman's position of poverty and dependence in the family was not recognized by many social investigators of the day.

Eleanor Rathbone MP, wanted an independent income for women with children.

Through the Family Endowment Society which Eleanor Rathbone set up in 1917, she campaigned for a system of Family Allowances paid by the State. A sum would be payable for the mother and each child. In this way Eleanor Rathbone felt that women would gain due recognition and respect for their role as mothers.

In 1929, Eleanor Rathbone entered Parliament as one of the first women MPs. She sat as an Independent MP until her death in 1946. In 1934 she set up another organization, the Children's Minimum Council, which aimed to set unemployment benefit at a level which could provide a decent diet for children. This, together with the Family Endowment Society, was the first pressure group for the family. At last, in 1945, the government agreed to pay Family Allowances – but Eleanor Rathbone still had to fight for the money to be paid to the mother rather than the father of the family.

Ever since 1945, the cash value of Family Allowances (now Child Benefit) has steadily declined. Eleanor Rathbone's campaign amounted to one of the very first calls for wages for housework. The fact that most later feminists have not taken up that call does not diminish her achievements.

> **Children are not simply a private luxury. They are an asset to the community, and the community can no longer afford to leave the provision for their welfare solely to the accident of individual income.** Eleanor Rathbone, *The Case for Family Allowances*, 1940.

7

Warfare and Welfare

1939–1959

Above *Land girls helped to run farms during the Second World War.*

Below *By the 1950s, typing and clerical work had become an acceptable occupation for women.*

Between the wars women had begun to work in a wider range of jobs, among them the expanding engineering industry, and the metal and chemical trades. Increasing numbers found clerical work as shorthand typists. In 1931, 34 per cent of women were in paid employment but still over a third of them were domestic servants. Of those women employed, 77 per cent were single, 16 per cent were married and 7 per cent were widowed or divorced. Married women were still barred from many occupations, including the civil service, banking, retailing and teaching.

When the Second World War (1939–1945) broke out, women went into paid employment on a much larger scale than in the First World War. Between 1939 and 1945, 1.5 million women

In 1942 working women were given time off from their jobs to do the shopping.

took jobs in engineering, chemicals, transport, and munitions as well as in the commercial sectors. This did not include the 470,000 women who had joined the armed forces by 1943. As most single women were already working before the war, a large number of the extra workforce were married women including those with young children. In 1943, 43 per cent of women in paid employment were married and 33 per cent of these had children under fourteen.

As a result, the government had to provide child care if they wanted mothers to work. Before the war, nurseries were only provided for badly deprived children, so there was a certain shame attached to the idea of state nurseries. The new wartime nurseries set up by the Ministry of Health were presented as healthy and good for the child as well as being geared to the needs of the working mother. For the first time you could be a good mother and leave your child in the nursery while you went out to work. In 1940 there were only fourteen state-run nurseries, but by 1943 this had expanded to 1,345.

More women were still needed in the workforce, but the government found that many women were reluctant to take jobs when they still had so many domestic responsibilities. Shopping and cooking meals were major problems for working women as there were no convenience foods or supermarkets. Workplace canteens and school meals helped, but they only provided a midday meal. Basic shopping had to be fitted into the working day, which was often impossible as many shops

This emphasis on women's role at home not only stressed the importance of bringing up children but also urged wives to be sympathetic and supportive to their husbands, whilst taking care to maintain men's conviction of their own superiority, and status as head of the family. April Carter, The Politics of Women's Rights, 1988.

> *For most of the nineteenth century and early twentieth century, only young single women ventured to do battle in the economic jungle. Gradually but most importantly after World War II work came to dominate a major part of a woman's life. Rather than being viewed as a separate stage, more often a stepping stone to marriage, it has become an integral aspect of many women's lives.* Patricia Branca, *Women in Europe Since 1750*, 1978.

still closed during lunch hours. In 1942 the Ministry of Labour recognized the problem and instructed employers to allow women time off work for shopping.

During the war, many families were disrupted by the evacuation programme which began in 1939. The government expected heavy bombing of highly populated towns by the Germans, so they moved children away from their homes in places like London, Liverpool and Birmingham, and sent them to country areas where they would be safer. In these areas they were sent to stay with local families. Sometimes they went with one of their parents, but often they went alone. Many evacuees came from poor homes and were not always welcomed by their host families who found them dirty and badly behaved. City children did not always find it easy to live in the country and they missed their families badly. Although evacuation made it easier for women with families to work, many found it a great hardship to be without their children for so long.

Children were evacuated from large cities to the countryside to avoid bombing in the Second World War.

After the war the legal gains made by women were less dramatic than in 1918. The main progress was in the removal of marriage bars to most occupations. Middle-class women could now pursue their career after marriage if they wished. The setting up of the Welfare State did improve women's lives, however, with the provision of free health care, family allowances and better council housing.

As soon as the war ended the wartime nurseries closed and women who had been so much in demand in the workforce found they were no longer required. There was a major campaign in women's magazines and in the press for women to return to a domestic life. After all the disruption and separation of the war years, many people felt that families needed to be rebuilt and there was also pressure to increase the falling population figures. Women were encouraged to enjoy making a home and were advised to put their families first.

The attractions of home life were easier to demonstrate as living standards improved and household appliances began to make life easier for the housewife. By 1949, 79 per cent of households had a gas supply and 86 per cent had electricity. Domestic work was still physically exhausting and time-consuming, but ownership of labour saving devices was beginning to increase. In 1948, 19 per cent of households had an electric cooker, 15 per cent had a water heater, but only 4 per cent had washing machines and 2 per cent owned a refrigerator. After the war cheap domestic help was less easily available, and consequently, many middle-class women found they were expected to do their own housework for the first time.

During the 1950s, attitudes to child care changed radically and emphasised the importance of a strong emotional bond between mother and child. Child care experts such as John Bowlby stressed the trauma and psychological damage caused by separation from the mother in the early years of life. All this made it difficult for women to go out to work without feeling guilty. Later on, working mothers were blamed for the rise in juvenile delinquency, as it was assumed that their children were neglected 'latch-key' kids.

What made most difference to women's lives at this time was the lower birth rate and their own increasing life-expectancy. Women now spent a far smaller part of their lives in child-bearing and so had time and energy to think about life outside the family. Social attitudes of the time, however, stressed the importance of full-time mothering and the virtues of being a good housewife. For these reasons most women felt unable to take advantage of the new circumstances.

In the 1950s, more labour-saving devices began to appear in homes. Adverts like this one from 1958 helped to change people's expectations.

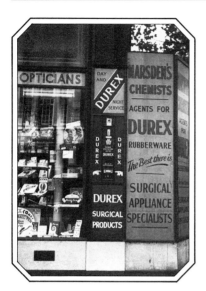

During the 1960s, contraception of all types became more socially acceptable and easily available.

8

Families and Jobs – The Double Burden

1960 onwards

During the 1950s, birth control for married women became more respectable and widely available. Voluntary groups such as the Family Planning Association opened new clinics all over the country. The Church of England now approved the use of contraception within marriage. Contraception for unmarried women was first available through the Brook Advisory Centres from 1964 onwards. In 1967, the passing of the Family Planning Act allowed local authorities to provide contraceptive services to unmarried people. This was a sign of major changes in the country's social attitudes.

In the early 1960s the contraceptive 'pill' was developed. This revolutionized contraception as it was reliable and easy to use. The pill gave women the freedom to enjoy sex without worrying about pregnancy. In 1967 the Abortion Law was changed so that a pregnancy could be terminated on the National Health Service as long as two doctors gave their consent. Legal abortion put an end to back street abortionists, who were estimated to have carried out 100,000 abortions per year before the law was changed. There was opposition to the new law from many sources, but it gave women new freedom to control their own bodies. In 1974 free contraception became available on the National Health Service and was now supplied by a woman's doctor.

Despite the use of contraception, the population was still growing and the average family size had remained more or less constant between 1958 and 1972 at 2.4 children per family. After 1971 the birth rate did begin to fall.

The number of illegitimate births was also rising at this time, from 4.8 per cent of total births in 1951 to 8.2 per cent in 1968. Although abortion and birth control for the unmarried became more widely available after this time, the number of children born outside marriage continued to increase. Today 17 per cent of babies are illegitimate, but this reflects changing social attitudes which make it more acceptable to have children without marrying.

Throughout this period many more women took up paid employment. A government survey carried out in 1980 showed that 66 per cent of women had jobs, although some worked part-time (26 per cent). Despite the fact that women now made up 40 per cent of the workforce, their working lives followed a very different pattern from that of male workers. Women work when their domestic commitments allow and their work has to fit in around family life. Women now return to work much sooner after having children, but many experience problems with child care as there is very little nursery provision in Britain. Hopes that employers would set up workplace nurseries to attract female workers have still not been fulfilled. Men who take time off to look after their children are still the exception rather than the rule. The part-time nature of women's work, punctuated by breaks for child care, means that many women are poorly paid and rarely reach the more senior posts.

Under pressure from the European Community, some laws were introduced in the 1970s which attempted to improve women's standing at work and in other spheres of life.

The Sex Discrimination Act (1975) opened up wider opportunities for women. Jo Atkins was the first woman to train as a Civil Engineer for Lewisham Borough Council.

The Equal Pay Act of 1970 required employers to pay men and women equal pay for equal work. As the Act did not come into force until 1975, however, many employers avoided paying women more by ensuring that their jobs were slightly different from men's. In 1975, the Sex Discrimination Act was passed. This prevented employers from refusing a job to a person simply because of their sex. It widened job opportunities for many women who wanted to work in jobs traditionally held by men. The Equal Opportunities Commission was set up to ensure the Act worked properly.

Although these legal changes did not rule out inequality for women at work they did enable women, in theory, to operate on an equal basis with men in the workplace. Most of the inequalities women now faced concerned their responsibility for child care and domestic work.

During the 1960s the divorce rate, which had been increasing since the turn of the century, began to soar. Between 1951 and 1968 the number of divorces granted each year doubled to 50,000. In 1980, 160,000 divorces were granted. Seven out of ten of these were granted to women. Part of the increase was due to legal changes which made divorce easier. In 1969 the Divorce Reform Act simplified divorce, and in 1970 the Matrimonial Proceedings and Property Act allowed women to claim a share in the family home when a marriage broke up.

Jo Richardson MP. In 1977, her Domestic Violence Act secured some protection for women with violent husbands.

A London branch of Gingerbread – a self-help group set up to give support to one-parent families.

The rising divorce rate does not necessarily mean that families are now less happy than they were. In the past many women had no choice but to stay in an unhappy marriage as they could not support themselves financially and the legal obstacles to obtaining a divorce were considerable. Changes in attitudes to divorce have meant that there is now less shame involved in ending a marriage.

One result of the rising number of divorces is that there are now more single-parent families than ever before. Some of these families are unmarried mothers bringing up their children alone, and some parents are alone as a result of the death of a partner, but the vast majority are in that situation because a marriage has broken up. Most single parents are women. Coping with a family single-handed can be very hard as all the practical and financial responsibilities fall on one adult. Social problems such as poverty and homelessness are far more common among single parents, as lack of child care facilities often makes it difficult for them to work. Groups such as 'Gingerbread' have been set up to provide much-needed support for one-parent families, but there is little practical support from government or welfare services.

In the 1970s there was increased public awareness of violence within marriage. Many women could not escape violent husbands because they had nowhere to go. Erin Pizzey pioneered the idea of refuges for battered women, allowing them an opportunity to break free.

> **6**
> *Greater belief in the importance of individual self-fulfilment and happiness, and less commitment to the concept of duty and the sanctity of family life, encouraged individuals to seek divorce and meant greater social tolerance for divorced women.* April Carter, *The Politics of Women's Rights,* 1988.
> **9**

Erin Pizzey (b.1939)

In 1971, Erin Pizzey and a group of local women took over a semi-derelict house in Chiswick to use as a women's centre. They decorated the house and it became a meeting place for young mothers who felt threatened and isolated in their homes. As a result of publicity the centre received in the newspapers and media, women began to arrive seeking shelter from their violent husbands. This first refuge for battered women drew attention to the problem, and the scale of marital violence became clearer.

In the 1970s, the Women's Aid Federation continued Erin Pizzey's pioneering work, by setting up 150 refuges nation-wide. In 1978 the Government asked the Women's Aid Federation to compile a survey about their work. They found that between 1977 and 1978 nearly 12,000 women and 21,000 children had stayed at the refuges and many more had been turned away as there was no room for them. The women had left their homes in order to escape physical violence to themselves and their children by their husbands. The attacks ranged from kicks and punches to attempted strangulation and knife wounds.

Many of the women had tried to leave home before (on average three times) but had no safe place to go to. Many of the

Erin Pizzey, who set up the first refuges for battered women and their children.

refuges were in a bad state of repair with inadequate space and facilities, and funding them was difficult.

In 1977 Jo Richardson MP introduced the Domestic Violence Act which allowed a woman to get a court injunction against her husband to prevent him from assaulting her. Although this helped some women it was difficult to enforce in an emergency. Many women were injured before they could get help.

Refuges for battered woman are an essential escape route for those in violent relationships, but there is still a need for better facilities and the provision of long-term housing by local councils.

> **Violence in the streets – straight thuggery and mugging – is treated as a serious crime... If the same act is committed behind the front door it is ignored.** Erin Pizzey, *Scream Quietly or the Neighbours Will Hear*, 1974.

9

Looking Forward to Equality at Home

The 1980s onwards

In the 1980s conditions for women with families became better than ever before. Although the struggle for legal and social equality over the last 200 years had been long and slow, women faced a much brighter future than that available to their grandmothers. This chapter reviews some of the benefits women experienced during the 1980s.

After falling in the mid-1970s, the birth rate in the 1980s rose slightly as women in their thirties, who had postponed motherhood for career reasons, now began to have children. Smaller families became the norm. In 1986 the average family had 1.8 children.

Life expectancy for women rose from 52 years in 1901 to 77 years in 1986. The infant mortality rate was 9.5 per thousand in 1986, compared with 160 per thousand in 1900. This marked improvement was due to better nutrition, medical care, and living conditions.

At the beginning of the century marriage was almost the only way for a woman to survive. Outside marriage she faced poverty (due to the poor choice of jobs available to women) and an attitude of pity and condescension. During the 1980s, the number of marriages decreased and the divorce rate continued to rise – from 2 divorces per thousand married couples in 1961 to 13 per thousand in 1986. Women were at last able to escape from unhappy marriages.

The proportion of old people in the population increased (18 per cent are now over retirement age), adding to the burden of younger women who take responsibility for the care of their elderly relatives. Only 5 per cent of old people are looked after in institutions.

For the majority of families, housing has greatly improved during this century, and this has made a huge difference to women because the domestic work they do is so dependent on the amenities of the home. In 1989, 60 per cent of families owned their own home, and 97 per cent of households had their own bathroom and an inside toilet. This is a much brighter

Would you be more careful if it was you that got pregnant?

Contraception is one of the facts of life.
Anyone, married or single, can get free advice on contraception from their doctor or family planning clinic. You can find your local clinic under Family Planning in the telephone directory or Yellow Pages.

The Family Planning Information Service

This Family Planning Association poster cleverly brings home the point that contraception is not just the woman's responsibility.

❛ **A woman who has made it to the top today has usually done so by proving she was the 'best man for the job'. This is not difficult while she has the same flexibility as a man but once she has children it is harder for her to compete. Unless there are changes in the rigid patterns which govern most senior posts or a transformation of domestic routine, there will continue to be a scarcity of women at the top.** Angela Holdsworth, *Out of the Doll's House*, 1988. ❜

A shortage of Council housing means many homeless families have to live in bed-and-breakfast accommodation.

picture than the one described by Margery Spring Rice in 1939 when only 10 per cent of families had their own indoor cold water tap. Ownership of domestic appliances has continued to increase, so that at the end of the 1980s nearly every household had a television and fridge, and 81 per cent of households had a washing machine and telephone. All these facilities make life easier for women as they minimize housework, cleaning and washing.

Not all groups, however, have been able to share in the general improvement in living standards. The high unemployment of the 1980s, particularly in the north and inner cities, meant that many families had to rely on state benefits and live in bad housing. The problem of homelessness also rose during the 1980s as council housing was sold to tenants, leaving a smaller stock of accommodation for those in need. Homeless families are now housed in single room bed-and-breakfast hotels which

Good child care is often expensive and hard to find, which makes it difficult for mothers to work. These under-fives enjoy lunch at the Tower Hamlets nursery.

are expensive and unsuitable for bringing up children. Women coping with these circumstances find life very hard indeed.

Ethnic minority groups also experience more than their share of poverty and hardship. Although the non-white population of Britain is only 4 per cent of the total, they are generally concentrated in the deprived inner city areas. Forty per cent of the West Indian and Asian population were born in Britain, but they still face discrimination in jobs and housing.

A very high proportion of West Indian women go out to work (70 per cent) and this causes many problems relating to child care. Asian women are less likely to be in employment, but many do outwork at home or in sweatshops in the fashion industry. This work is generally very poorly paid.

Contraception changed during the 1980s as the Pill was found to be linked to certain forms of cancer. With the advent of AIDS the use of condoms became more widespread. But the

Although some men do now share the housework, most domestic chores are still done by women.

contraception problem is not entirely solved. Many married couples who have had as many children as they want turn to sterilization as a long-term solution.

Smaller families and more labour-saving facilities in the home have made it easier for women to work, and this has brought them a measure of financial independence. However, many women still find it difficult to go out to work because of their domestic responsibilities and the lack of child care facilities. Some employers have begun to consider providing workplace nurseries, and population changes in the early 1990s, which will mean a shortage of school leavers, may persuade companies to provide child care to attract women back to work.

Housework, although much less arduous than in the early years of the century, still falls heavily upon women. The participation of men in housework and child care has changed very little during the 200 years this book has covered.

Women may enjoy a more equal relationship with men in many ways, but in the majority of homes the traditional family tasks are still done by women. Until this domestic burden is more evenly shared, women must wait for equality in the home.

Project

The aim of this project is to find out as much as you can about the daily routine experienced by women in the past and to understand how it has changed in recent times. There are many sources of information on this topic:

Books – these may be historical accounts (such as that written by John Seymour, *Forgotten Household Crafts*) or they may be old household manuals – Isabella Beetham's *The Book of Household Management* (1861). These gave housewives instruction in how to run a home efficiently. An elderly friend or relative may have one you could borrow or you might find one at a second-hand bookshop. Old magazines can also supply interesting information. Cynthia White has compiled a book entitled *Women's Magazines 1693-1968* which your local library may be able to get for you. Ask the librarian to help.

Museums – some museums and old houses have exhibitions about daily life in the past and many have examples of tools and equipment used in housework. If the museum has an Education Officer, she or he may be able to help you find out more.

Interviews with elderly relatives or friends – for more recent history (this century) a good way to find out about how housework was done is to ask people to remember their own lives. Try to find someone who was a domestic servant or housewife before 1939. It is a good idea to organize your questions clearly before-

hand and to use a tape recorder. Here are some suggestions for topics on which to base your questions:

Cleaning and Washing:
How were floors and carpets cleaned?
How was washing-up done?
How was water collected for cleaning and washing?
How was water heated?
What equipment was used for washing?
How long did a weekly wash take and how was it dried?

Shopping and Cooking:
How often did you shop for meat and vegetables?
What type of shops sold basic foods?
How was food brought home?
How was it stored?
What equipment was used for cooking?
What type of fuel did the cooker use?

Heating and Lighting:
How was the home heated?
What extra work was required to keep the home warm?
What kind of lighting did the house have?

When you have collected enough answers, write a short report about *Housework in the Past* and then you could write another piece about how you expect your own house to be run during the next 10-15 years. Include the machines you would use and the facilities you would expect to have. This will give a useful comparison showing how the burden of housework has changed during the last hundred years.

Books to Read

Books for younger readers

Davies, Margaret Llewellyn *Maternity: Letters from working women* (Virago, 1978)*

Holdsworth, Angela *Out of the Doll's House* (BBC Books, 1988)

Hughes, Molly *A London Child of the 1870's*, *A London Girl of the 1880's* and *A London Home of the 1890's* (Oxford University Press, 1979)*

Hyndley, Kate *Let's Discuss Family Life* (Wayland, 1988)

Reeves, Maud Pember *Round About a Pound a Week* (Virago, 1979)*

Rice, Margery Spring *Working Class Wives* (Virago, 1981)*

Samuel, Raphael *East End Underworld* (Routledge and Kegan Paul, 1981)*

Seymour, John *Forgotten Household Crafts* (Dorling Kindersley, 1987)

*These books contain personal accounts which give an easy-to-read overall impression of women's lives in the past.

Books for older readers

Beddoe, Deirdre *Discovering Women's History* (Pandora, 1983)

Braybon, Gail *Women Workers in the First World War* (Croom Helm, 1981)

Carter, April *The Politics of Women's Rights* Longman, 1988)

Hardyment, C. *From Mangle to Microwave: mechanisation of the household* (Polity Press, 1988)

Lewis, Jane *Women in England 1870–1950* (Wheatsheaf Books, 1984)

Oakley, Anne *Housewife* (Penguin, 1976)

Summerfield, Penny *Women Workers in the Second World War* (Croom Helm, 1986)

White, Cynthia *Women's Magazines 1693–1968* (Michael Joseph, 1970)

Glossary

Access The right of each parent to be allowed to visit or take turns in looking after their children, after separation or divorce.

Adultery Sexual intercourse of a married person with someone other than their husband or wife.

'Angel in the home' An idea that came to prominence during the Victorian period (1837–1901). The poet Coventry Patmore described a woman's true role as the 'angel in the home' – where she had to strive to be the perfect lady, perfect wife and perfect mother.

Annulled Cancelled, declared invalid.

Ante-natal services Health care for pregnant women before their babies are born.

Birth control Methods of preventing unwanted pregnancy.

Birth rate Number of births per 1,000 population.

Black-leaded A fire grate or cooking range polished with graphite to leave a deep shine.

Census Official survey of the population giving information about how many people exist, where they live, and the work they do.

Condom A rubber sheath which is placed over the man's penis prior to sexual intercourse. It is a popular, safe form of contraception.

Conscription Compulsory membership of the armed forces.

Contraception *See birth control.

Deprived Lacking adequate food, shelter and education.

Divorce rate Number of divorces per 1,000 married couples.

Domestic service Working as a household servant.

Domestic work Work done in the home, as part of running a household.

Dr Barnardo's Home A charity, which houses homeless children.

Evacuation Taking people away from danger zones in wartime.

Family Allowance Payment made by the State to the parents of a child or children, to help with the cost of looking after a family. Similar to modern-day Child Benefit.

Feminist A person who believes in equality for women.

Gentility Affected politeness.

Gingerbread Group A voluntary organization providing support for one-parent families.

Guardian A person who has legal responsibility for a child.

Gynaecologist A doctor specializing in women's health.

Gynaecology The branch of medicine concerned with women's health problems.

Health visitors Trained nurses who advise mothers in their own homes about childcare, nutrition and health.

Illegitimate A child born to unmarried parents.

Independent MP An MP who is not affiliated to a particular political party.

Industrial Revolution A period of British history starting around the 1760s, in which the invention of a series of machines and implements led to a revolution in the way goods were made.

Infant mortality The number of babies who die before they are one year old, per 1,000 babies born.

Juvenile delinquency Law-breaking by young offenders.

Life expectancy The number of years, on average, a person can expect to live.

Maintenance Money to live on paid by one partner of a marriage to the other when a marriage breaks up.

Marriage bar A rule preventing married women from working in particular jobs.

Maternal mortality The number of mothers who die in childbirth per 1,000 babies born.

Munitions factories Factories where weapons and ammunition are made.

Non consummation A marriage which is not legally complete because sexual intercourse has not taken place.

Philanthropist A person who tries to help others through charity and other acts of good will.

Poor Law A means of helping the poor and destitute who could not support themselves.

Psychological Relating to psychology – the scientific study of all forms of human behaviour.

Sanitation A way of removing sewage and rubbish so that healthy conditions can exist without dirt and disease.

Single-parent family A family consisting of children living with only one parent, usually the mother.

Socialist A person who believes in socialism – whereby a country's wealth (land, industry, resources) should belong to the people, not to private owners, and the state should decide how such resources are used for the common good.

Sterilization An operation which makes the female reproductive organs cease to function.

Stillbirth A baby which is born dead.

Women's liberation movement A movement developing in the late 1960s in America and moving to Britain in the early 1970s, which sought to end discrimination against women in all areas of life.

White collar Non-manual work as in clerical or secretarial jobs.

Index

Numbers that are printed in **bold** indicate illustrations.

Abortion 36
  Abortion Law (1967) 36
  'Angel in the home' 4, 5, 14

Battered women 39, 40
Birth control 25, **25,** 26, 30, 36, **36, 41,** 43
Birth rate 4, 5, 22, 34, 41, 44
Bodichon, Barbara 17, **17**
Bowlby, John 35
Brook Advisory Centres 36

Cheltenham Ladies College 18
Child care 9, 11, 33, 35, 37, 39, 43, 44
Child labour 9, **10**
Contraception *see birth control*
Cottage industry 8, 9, **9**

Davies, Margaret Llewellyn 23
Divorce 4, 11, 14, 28, 38–9
Divorce Reform Act (1969) 38
Domestic service 7, **7,** 15, 27
Domestic Violence Act (1977) 40

Education **17,** 18, **18**
Mrs Ellis 14, 16
  Daughters of England 14
Equal opportunities **37**
Equal Opportunities Commission 38
Equal Pay Act 38
Ethnic minorities 43
Evacuation 34, **34**

Fabian Women's Group 23, 24
  Round About a Pound a Week 23
Family Allowances 30, 31, 34
Family Planning Association 36

First World War 17, 18, 24, 27, 28, 32

Gingerbread 39
Guardianship of Infants Act (1886) 17
Guardianship of Infants Act (1925) 28

Harding, Arthur 19, 20
Health care 22, 29, 30
  nutrition 23, 24, 41
  midwives 28
Hill, Octavia 20
Housework 5, 6, 11, 15, 34, 42, 44, **44**
Housing 20, 24, 30, 41, **42**
  homelessness 42
Hughes, Molly 18, 19
  A London Girl of the 1880s 18

Industrial Revolution 4, 8, 9, **11**
Infants' Custody Act 12

Labour saving devices 6, **6, 29,** 34, 35

Marriage 8, 10, 13, 14, 41
  legal status 7, 11, 17, 27
  and work 32, 33, 34
Married Women's Property Act (1882) 17
Maternity and Child Welfare Act 28
Matrimonial Women's Proceedings and Property Act (1970) 38
Middle-class women 10, 11, 14, 34

National Insurance Act (1911) 22
National Society for Prevention of Cruelty to Children (NSPCC) 24

New Poor Law (1834) 16
Norton, Caroline 11, 12, **12,** 28
Nurseries **28,** 33, 34, 37, **43,** 44

Pizzey, Erin 39, 40, **40**
Poverty 15, **16**
  workhouses 16

Queen Victoria 14

Rathbone, Eleanor 30, **30,** 31
Reeves, Maud Pember 23
Rice, Margery Spring 29, 39
  Working Class Wives 29
Richardson, Jo **38,** 40

Sanitation 15
Second World War 7, 32
Sex Discrimination Act 38
Single-parent families 39
Stopes, Marie 25, 26, **26**
  Married Love 26
  Wise Parenthood 26
Suffrage 17, 27

Unemployment 15, 27, 42
Unemployment benefit 31
Upper-class families **13**
Upper-class women 11

War work **21, 22, 23,** 24
Washing **14,** 15, 20, **20,** 30, 42
Welfare State 34
Widows 16
Women's Co-operative Guild 23
Working-class women 9, 10, 14, 15